Table of Contents

Introduction

Your Customers Hold the Key to Your Success

What are the secrets to holding on to and attracting even more great customers? And once you have great customers, what is your strategy? Do you have a systematic way to attract and hold on to really great customers? We do it through Kick-Ass Customer Service.

First, the Bad News: You are losing some good customers.

The Good News: You don't need to lose them.

More Bad News: You are wasting time and money trying to buy your customers. The Good News: You can stop doing that NOW.

More Good News: It is far more effective to implement Kick-Ass Customer Service Principles than to beg your customers to return, wonder about Facebook, kiss ass or pay thousands more for ineffective advertising.

This book is about how customer service makes a difference, how paying attention to your customers, actually finding out what they want, and being creative and open to simple but effective ways to add value, can make a huge difference in your business, effectively transforming it. And I mean *any* business.

A note before we begin: There are slight differences between the words clients and customers. For *the purposes of this book, I will be using the term "customer" to include clients*. The people who keep you in business are your customers, and we'll help you connect with them and build those long-term relationships you need to succeed. This book is about transforming your business by putting your customers first—whether you work in travel, construction, hot beverages, or anything in between.

Ready?

Chapter 1

Do You Know What Your Customer Really Wants?

The easiest way to begin to make a customer happy is to ask them what they want. A lot of businesses assume and mostly neglect to ask their customers what they want first. To truly give customer service that creates a long-term relationship with a client, one of the first things you want to do is focus on them and ask them what they want.

Whether it's how they want their coffee made, if they like a certain room in your hotel, their favorite time of day to take hot air balloon rides, or a particular type of wine—whatever it may be—ask them what it is that they want.

Why?

Because when you ask your customer to focus on what they want *first*, it allows both of you to get organized around where they are going, and not where they've been, and it helps create a clear and compelling idea in your mind and in the minds of those around you about what to do next.

You want your customers to devote *at least* 50% of their time to talking about what they want and creating a mental picture so that you both have a clear understanding of what you can do for them. If you want a satisfied customer, it helps to know a few specifics.

By learning what the customer wants first, you avoid a common pitfall. A lot of people are used to discussing the problem first. That is moving backward. The vast majority of people know what the problems are in any given situation. But when we focus on the problem first, we're headed in the wrong direction. When we focus on what went before we can get caught up in what we don't want. If you want to experience the difference, just for 10 seconds or so focus on something you don't want. Done? Good, now focus for 10 seconds on something you really want. Notice how different those two feelings can be!

In a room full of people, the leaders are generally the people who have a vision (yes, a picture in their mind) and know where they want to go. The leaders aren't the people complaining about what has gone before, the mistakes that were made, or the problems. You want to make sure you start out by helping your customer to clearly understand what they want.

It becomes your job to help them get what they want. Just be sure that you are absolutely certain that you know before you begin to offer your solutions. This is really the key to a successful business relationship—that is, helping your customer to clearly state what they want. It can be magical.

In a larger sense, it's the leader in the room who talks about solutions and is able to communicate that in a clear vision. The leader paints the picture and works on it until people begin to understand what that picture is. A leader organizes everybody around a solution rather than a problem.

When you work with your customer toward a solution, they will see you as the leader who can help solve their problems.

Although it may seem strange at first, spend very little time on the customer's present situation, the one they want to change. The present situation isn't where you're headed with your customer—that's where you're starting from, and if you want to make progress, you need to move forward, toward a solution.

When you have a clear picture of what your customer wants, then you can move on to the next step: developing an action plan.

Your action plan must have these four components:

1. Solution—the final outcome you and your client desire. What your customer wants.
2. Starting point—where are you at the moment.
3. Strategy—how to get from where you are to where you want to be.
4. Action—doing the work to get to where you want to be.

Delegate and make assignments of different action steps for you, your partners and your employees to take. Set a timeline and begin the process.

To provide Kick-Ass Customer Service, you must first become the leader your customers are looking for. Remember that you become the leader by carefully listening. Once you know what your customer wants, you can start working toward a solution. Implementing this single step has the power to transform your business seemingly overnight—and it all starts with finding out *exactly* what your customer wants.

Chapter 2

Would You Rather Have Employees or Ambassadors?

So few operations, in the grand scheme of things, treat their customers with the kind of respect and service that gets those customers to really feel noticed and respected, and therefore come back. Although *you* know to look for solutions with your customers, you also know that you will not always be the face your customers see. Whether they're answering the phone, laying out merchandise, conducting inventory or pouring coffee, your employees represent your company almost as often as you do.

With that in mind, it's in your and your customers' best interests to entrust your employees with the skills and belief in the company that help them put the customer first.

Rather than just allowing people to be run-of-the-mill employees, you want to empower them to be more professional and helpful. Ambassadors are a great example. Ambassadors serve their constituency, and when your employees begin to think like ambassadors, they are welcoming customers to your business as opposed to just staffing a store. It's a different, and more important, way to think about doing business.

There are many reasons it's more productive to work with ambassadors than with employees, and here are just a few:

- Ambassadors think of the customer first.
- Ambassadors focus on what they can contribute to the business.
- An ambassador is not about being a salesperson; it's about being of service.
- An Ambassador will educate first (more on this important concept later).
- Ambassadors have authority to introduce customers to different services and products.
- Ambassadors model a professional, helpful and respectful tone.

If you're convinced that your employees should be ambassadors of your business, the next question should be: "How can I make that happen?"

You don't necessarily need to *call* them ambassadors, but you do have to *show* them how to act as ambassadors. No matter what role they serve in the company, a critical part of their job is attracting new customers. There are several ways to make the transition to ambassadors, and it's important to keep your goal in mind as you implement the strategies.

One last note before we begin: Before you ask anyone else to take these steps, it is crucial that you model the behaviors and practices you want them to implement. Your ambassadors must always be able to look to you for the example to follow.

And that's part of the first step—inspire your employees to become ambassadors to your customers. By treating your employees with the respect they deserve, and modeling the way to treat others, they will convey that feeling to your customers. You'll know you're making progress when they want to come back to work, or stay the extra hour you ask them to. Maybe they'll work on a Saturday when they weren't supposed to. An ambassador is invested in the success of their business, and when they feel like they are important to the success of the business, they will not only do more for you, but they will also advertise that feeling to everyone they come in contact with.

The next step is to teach them about focusing on solutions, as we discussed in the first chapter. When a customer arrives in the place of business, ambassadors will be completely focused on ensuring that the customer's needs and wants are addressed and met. That can be applied to every aspect of any role within your company.

A respected customer is one who feels noticed and appreciated, as well as someone who comes back and tells their friends about your service.

Imagine the job is answering the phone. An ambassador is sincerely happy to hear from a customer and focuses attention on what that phone call is about so that customer is better served. In every moment, an ambassador is very carefully listening and thinking, "What is the solution that we can work together to get for this person?" Instead of wondering what a customer's pro*bl*em is, an ambassador is looking to find solutions and enhance their experience. It becomes a model for how any customer can and should be treated. We'll talk more at the end of this chapter on Phone Magic and how to create it in your business.

Once people become ambassadors, it sets them apart from employees at other businesses, and they also begin to enjoy it. The day is a lot more productive and fun when we enjoy what we're doing. Ambassadors' jobs become not only more valuable to the company but actually easier to do. It's more opportunity, and it's added value for the customer and the employee. The more you treat your employees at that higher level, the more your customers will feel that higher level of service and respect, and the more value your employees bring to the business. It's a rewarding cycle where everybody wins.

This experience is also something an employee can take anywhere they go in life. If they enter another line of work, they are going to have that much more value going into the new job—they'll be an authority of sorts on how to treat customers.

How can ambassadors inspire customers to bring their friends?

There's a reason it's called customer service—you're giving your customers something they didn't have when they walked in the door, whether they purchase anything from you or not. Notice your customer and pay attention. Ask their name and introduce yourself. Listen to them. Find out why they're there.

Next, follow up. Did you exceed your customer's expectations? Is there something you could have done to make their experience just a little more enjoyable? Keep in mind that what your customer wants, what they will report to their friends and associates, is the experience they had. This is the feedback you're going to need to move forward and create those long-term relationships for your business's success.

If your customer is satisfied, review what you've done and make sure to apply it in the future. But if your customer has a complaint, you have an even greater opportunity to excel. Complaints are one of the best places to practice Kick-Ass Customer Service, and the way you treat your customer through this process could very well motivate them to tell their friends about your products or services.

When people complain, that's a real test to see if you are up to the task of taking care of them. I want to use an example to best show the difference stellar customer service can make:

Let's say you run a window-cleaning business, and you've just completed a big, beautiful house with lots of huge windows. The lady of the house says to you, "You know, this window didn't really get as clean as the rest." Is your immediate response to say the window was dirtier than you expected or to discuss the warranty or guarantee of your work? No, that is focusing on the past. Once you start that conversation, you've probably already lost that customer for good. Ask your customer exactly what they would like. If you are clear that you're there to serve them and you want them happy, you'll probably say, "I'm sorry! We'll fix this right away at no charge." And do what you say. With a response focused on Kick-Ass Customer Service, you've just turned that customer into not only a repeat client, but someone who will tell her friends and neighbors about the excellent service you provided. If you're willing to take on the job at all, you want your customers happy. Provide an experience that makes certain they will be.

Don't worry about scammers in this situation. One company I consult for is a carpet company, and early on in their marketing process, I said, "What I want you to do is give a 100% money-back guarantee: If you're dissatisfied for any reason, we won't charge you." It's been about a year and a half now, and, at this writing, they have never once lost money on that guarantee because they have always strived to give their customers the best service possible. If you do a great job and your customer appreciates it, they'll tell two, three, four other people how responsive you were and what great service you gave. It is a *great* strategy for getting your customers to do some free advertising for you.

What Is Phone Magic and Why Is It So Important to Your Success?

Your phone is a critical point of entry into your business, and there are ways you and your new ambassadors can use your phone that will make it a far more powerful resource in your business. I want to go over a few ways you can provide Kick-Ass Customer Service that will bring you more customers with every phone call you make and receive.

Stand Up While Talking: When you stand up, you have better posture. You also tend to be more relaxed and breathe easier, which helps you speak more clearly, contributing to a much more powerful way to speak. People can really hear over the phone that you're comfortable speaking with them and working toward a solution.

Smile: While you're standing up, one of the most important things you can do on the phone is smile. When you think about it, there aren't too many things that you can tell about a person on the other end of your call. Although they may not be able to see you, people really can hear if you're smiling. Try it! A smile really frames what your customer thinks about you. A smile while talking on the phone changes how people feel on the other end of the line. It's pretty magical in the way it can relax the person on the other end of the conversation. Smiles are also contagious and help to demonstrate subconsciously that you are at ease and enjoying what you're doing, all of which contributes to the image of you as an expert or authority on your subject. Breathing properly, standing up straight, and smiling all help to awaken all the right neurons in your brain and body.

Listen: The next thing you can do that's incredibly powerful is listen. Pay attention, and listen at least twice as much as you talk. You're listening carefully for what it is that your customer wants. Write down the three key points your phone partner is saying, even if that's just their name, phone number, and a short message. Then again, perhaps they'd like to rent a room at your inn, or they'd like to know what kind of wines you have, or perhaps they want to know if you have room at your restaurant for the number of people they are going to be bringing. Pay really close attention to the kinds of things they want and you'll be surprised at the effectiveness. There are many people who are incredibly effective on the phone, and they are successful just because of that.

Trust Yourself: Through all of this, remember to trust yourself. Relax into what you're doing. Trust that you know what you're doing. You'll have a much more successful, productive time on the phone with your customers. Keep in mind that it's the portal to your business. Smile, trust yourself, stand up, and breathe.

One Thing at a Time: Avoid multitasking when talking to a customer on the phone. Customers can tell, and it will speak volumes about how important they are to you.

Adopting these kick-ass strategies, and inspiring your new ambassadors to do the same, is a huge step toward transforming your business into a customer attraction machine. When you and your ambassadors are fully focused on providing great products, a great experience, and Kick-Ass Customer Service for your customers, employee service becomes customer service, which becomes—yes—more customers.

Chapter 3

Are You Educating or Just Selling?

I strongly suggest that the businesses I consult for educate, not sell. There are important differences between selling to your customer and educating them. If you're selling to somebody, it becomes a competition. You're trying to get them to buy and they're trying to get the lowest price. A competition means you're facing off with the customer; however, if you're educating, you're standing side by side with your customer and looking in the same direction for a *solution*. Think about it. Often, someone who is trying to sell to you will sit across from you at the table and you will be looking in opposite directions in the room. But someone who is effective at really helping you will sit next to you and you will be looking in the same direction together. Try it.

There's a built-in conflict with selling, but when you're educating them, there's a built-in partnership. When you're working together to find a solution, you become the expert, in a very helpful way.

The difference becomes clear at the beginning of the conversation. As we discussed in the first chapter, we always want to start by asking your customer what they want. The vast majority of businesses I know don't ask their customer what they want—they make the assumption, guess, or think about what's popular or what their experience is. But they usually never go out and ask them what it is they would like, or how it is they would like to receive it.

Next, focus at least 50% of your conversation helping them to clarify what it is they want. Once you're asking them what they want, try to not get into the position where they're talking about their problems. Try to get into the position, as we talked about before, where they're talking about what it is they want. Have them describe the map or the picture of what it is they want, the good or the service. If they can't get really clear about it in a picture, ask them what results they want. What results are they looking for? What outcome are they looking for? What feeling would they like to experience? Then work very diligently to make that a shared goal so that you can repeat it, at any time, to your sales force or to your employees. You should know it well enough so that you can make sure they get what they want.

What your customers want can be something as simple as an extra-hot, foamy cappuccino versus a dry not-so-hot cappuccino, or it could be something like a new car, or a night out, or a delicious wine. It can be just about anything. If you ask them about how they would like to have it, what solution they're looking for, and what experience they're looking for, then you're a long way toward being able to create that situation for your customer. And then once you've made it a shared vision, repeat it back to them. Say, for example, "What I understand is that you would like a wine, probably a red, that goes well with spaghetti."

When the picture of what your customer wants is crystal clear, something like magic happens. The pressure greatly lessens on you because when you've repeated it back to them and both of you are clear about what your customer wants, it's a little like magic—then you start to give it to them. Mostly you want to give your customer what they want, not what you think they need. If you think you know of a better choice you can respectfully suggest it to them. You can, if it is done carefully, educate them about how to add value to their choice.

Sometimes customers don't know what they want. In that case, you can help them along by asking, "Well, what's the outcome you want?" "What is the result you are looking for?" or "What is the experience you want to have?" As a leader, and as the service or product provider, you can tailor your questions and give details to help them find the product or service that suits them best. But it's important that you ask them what they want and get clear on it, because once you've done that, you've got a friend because you have really heard them and they will feel important. When you can ask for somebody's vision and give it to them, they're going to love you for it because so few people do that. You become not only an expert but also a very interesting person because you've somehow figured them out.

One of the reasons that Starbucks is so successful is because their customers very specifically order and receive exactly what they want. And it seemed so corny at first. And, even better, if they don't like what they get, they can exchange that drink for another. There is no doubt that getting your product or service the way you want it is a powerful way to get you to come back.

As with anything in your business, you want to be working toward a solution, and when it comes to educating your customers instead of selling them, it's yet another way you can demonstrate that you notice them, you're paying attention, and you can deliver what they want.

Becoming the expert to whom your customers turn is Kick-Ass Customer Service that helps your customers see you as a leader and transforms your business at the same time.

Chapter 4

What Is the Difference Between Gratitude and Appreciation?

People want to spend time where they feel welcome, and appreciating those who patronize your business is the simplest way to show customers how welcome they are. Your customers could have selected any other business to spend their money, but they have chosen yours for any number of reasons. Let them know the gratitude you feel for their great decision.

There are a few connotations out there for these two words. For me, gratitude is a very strong feeling of something that you really are thankful for, and appreciation is the expression of that gratitude. Another great definition of appreciation is "to grow in value." So when I really am grateful for something, I express my gratitude in the form of appreciation, and in doing that, I make my gratitude more valuable by sharing it. Does it really matter if I feel gratitude if I don't thank the people who give me that feeling? Sharing that feeling of gratitude by demonstrating your appreciation turbo-charges the experience. I add a great deal of value to the gratitude I feel when I share or express it.

You can use those feelings of gratitude and expressions of appreciation in your business in several ways. The first step for doing just that is noticing your customers, making eye contact, smiling, and saying, "Good morning," or "Good afternoon." Tell them you want them to feel welcome. Ask if there's anything you can do for them. This happens so infrequently that people can be just blown away by businesses that make the effort. And showing appreciation can be as simple as acknowledgement.

This doesn't have to be done in an obnoxious way. Showing appreciation can make people feel warm, even the people who don't want to be bothered in the morning. Just smiling at them in a welcoming way can make all the difference in the world in their day, even if they don't fully acknowledge it at first. It demonstrates that you and your business are alive.

Step two is feeling gratitude for the fact that they are your customers and that they're in your place of business. Just experiencing the gratitude for the fact that you've got this business, and there are people walking around and buying in it, is very powerful. And feeling the gratitude leads to the next logical step in the process.

Expressing your gratitude is step three. Tell your customers how much you appreciate them doing business with you. Let them know in a genuine way that you appreciate their business and that they're spending their hard-earned money with you. Make sure they know that you're willing to help them in any way and serve them in any way you know how. A business owner or business employee who will take the time out to acknowledge customers will notice a huge difference in the number of people that are in their business.

Step four is to look for a connection with your customer. They're in your business, so you have the first connection, but is there something less obvious? It could be the town you live in, a favorite sport, or a favorite product or service you provide that you're both enthusiastic about. Find out a little something about them and why they're there, and then you can do something really powerful. I've done this on a number of occasions for businesses I consult for—I started meeting customers that are in a business and introducing them to each other! It's remarkable. One morning you can walk into a place, let's say a coffee shop, and nobody's talking to each other. You start introducing people to each other and letting them know the common interests they share, and a week later you can walk in and they're sitting with each other. It's really fun, and it begins to build community, which is a very powerful social perk when you show your customers that it's safe to do so.

Another note is that people respond really well when you are way more *interested* than *interesting*. Talking to people about the big game hunting you did when you were a child is great—if it connects you to your customer. What's more important than what you're doing is what your customers are doing and finding ways to be interested by looking for the connection. So take a few moments, make sure your phone is off, ask them what brought them in, and cultivate a real level of genuine interest. Have a real conversation. You're going to see a significant return on investment when you're genuinely interested in your customers. Let your customers talk about who they are while you demonstrate who you are through Kick-Ass Customer Service.

Remember, you don't want to *buy* the connection; you want to *make* the connection. It's a nice thing to do to give a customer a free cup of coffee or comp their room now and again, but you really want to know who they are and why they're there. We have met some of the most interesting people in restaurants, vineyards and chiropractic offices just by talking to them and comparing notes. The connection is there, and it's your role to reveal it and strengthen it.

And finally, always remember to thank your customer. Remember to reveal your gratitude by showing appreciation. There are three important times when you're in contact with your customer: when they arrive, while they get their service or product, and when they leave. In all three places, they can be thanked. One of the places to thank them that can be very powerful is noticing when they're leaving and just really thanking them for coming. You don't have to wait until they're walking out the door; you can thank them for their business at any time. It's something that most businesses don't do, and the ones that do it often see a real uptick in people coming back . . . for the experience of being thanked!

Also, remember that you are always modeling this behavior for your employees.

As we discussed in the Ambassadors chapter, the people who work for you need to have an inspiring example to follow. Don't tell your employees what to do; show them how to do it. You are a model for the behavior your employees learn. Explain and then demonstrate the type of experience that you want your customers to have. For most employees, it's kind of daunting to go out and introduce themselves unless they're going to sell something, and you don't always want people selling—you want them serving and educating.

So, make sure your customers know how much you appreciate their business. When you acknowledge them, feel and express your gratitude, find a connection, and be more interested than interesting, customers will appreciate the business you have created even more. With these strategies, you will be talking to your customers in a way that makes them want to come back as well as talk to their friends about you, your products and service.

Chapter 5

Are You Offering Your Customers a Life-Enhancing or a Life-Changing Experience?

Your customers choose your business for more important reasons than just the product or service you offer. For example, if you own a coffee shop, people can stop at most any gas station if they just want a cup of coffee. But they've chosen your business for the *experience* of the whole visit, and even more so when it comes to higher-end items. The simplest way to find out about the experience they're looking for is to, in an appreciative way, ask them.

And listen to what they say. Once you begin to find out why your customers continue to be your customers, at least two different things are going to happen. One is you're going to get a really great understanding of why people are coming to see you—and it may not be for the reasons you know about. And two, once you have that understanding, you can enhance their experience for them.

As the business owner, or even as an employee, you have an enormous amount to do with the experience your customers are going to have. Whatever your product or service is, that's just the beginning of what is possible for you to serve your customer.

Show your customers that you're noticing them and that you're paying attention to them. Each time you interact with your customers, offer them something they're not going to necessarily get on an everyday basis with anybody else in your industry, or in any other business like yours. Just actively listening is great, or ask them how their presentation went at work, or find out how their kid's baseball game went. Your goal is to do something they really remember that makes their day better, or even changes their life. A big one is simply remembering their name.

Really pay attention and try to start a conversation, even if it's just a brief one.

With the customers who have been to your business many, many times, they know what they want. With your long-time, repeat customers, work a little bit harder to enhance their experience even more with your product or service. Notice if there is something special that you can do to enhance their experience. Ask them their opinion (Whoa!) about some aspect of your business that you know they have expertise in. Most people love being noticed and when you add a little something to remind them later on, they will share that experience with others.

How Do I Know Which Customers to Approach?

If you've never approached your customers before, start out with just approaching any of them and starting that one-on-one conversation. Tell them you appreciate their business, compliment them, and discuss what you can do to make their experience better.

This isn't something you can fake and this is not a change that most people can do overnight, but once you've learned and embraced this way of customer service, it can become a very valuable part of your day. I highly recommend it. Over time, you'll develop a feel for how to approach almost anybody. And what you'll learn from your customers about your business will be invaluable and help them to feel invested in your success.

Again, you want to make absolutely sure that you model this behavior for whomever you're going to have do it. If you want your employees to do this (and you should really consider the power in this), show them several examples of how to start these conversations so they can feel comfortable. Take them along while you are making your rounds. Once they learn this, you've shown them how they can be ambassadors, and they'll enjoy their time at work even more as well.

As you get down the road, you're going to find that there are certain people in your business who are just kind of the life of the party. You just really enjoy that they're there. These are the people you want to ask opinions of.

For example, I have a sports bar I really like visiting. And not just for the big screen TVs. I comment all the time on the changes they've made. And it's a very nice place. They've got fourteen big screen TVs in a relatively small space, they serve very tasty food at reasonable prices, the place is spotlessly clean, and they have great customer service. They are always trying to make their customers' experience more fun. I know I'm not the normal customer, and I've made a point of connecting with them. But what they've done in return is paid a lot of attention to me because they expect me to tell my friends about them. And they're right. I've taken a number of people there, including my clients to have a business lunch. There's a small group of people that go there now because I told them about it. All of this is because the people there have connected with me—they ask about my clients, my business, my life, and they show a real genuine interest. They go the extra mile to make it a place I want to tell everyone I know about.

There are certain types of questions you want to ask your customers, and a certain type you want to avoid. You want to find out the value they see in doing business with you—is it your incredible wine, food, balloon rides, or rooms? Is it for the community? Is it because your business was recommended to them by a friend or colleague? More good questions include:

- "When might we see you again?"
- "When was the last time you were here?"
- "How can we serve you?"
- "Who is your friend?"
- "How can we make your trip, your visit to our business, a little better?"
- "How has this product or service (experience) been working for you?"

And it doesn't hurt to write things down, either, so you can remember their answers (with their names!). You don't need to have a clipboard, but pull out a piece of paper. This is all about acknowledging people and making them feel noticed and appreciated—creating an experience they can associate with you and your business. You want each customer to feel important to the success of your business. When you continually make those connections, they will bring their friends to show them that they're important to your business.

The questions you might want to avoid in this situation are open-ended questions. These are very general questions with which you'll get any answer under the sun. Questions like, "How are you doing?" "Are you enjoying yourself?" You don't want to leave yourself wide open for complaints, particularly complaints you can't do anything about. You want to focus the question to allow people to talk about themselves in a way that's uplifting, moves the conversation forward, and focuses on what they want, not what they didn't get. Now, of course, you're going to get people who talk to you about their problems, but what you want to do is help them to refocus on what they want and how you can get them the experience they desire with your products or service. When you're moving forward like that, you're getting things done. You don't want to leave yourself open for a 30-minute conversation about a long-lost cat who's in the hospital. That just doesn't work for anybody in a business.

Focus on One Customer at a Time

Unless you're one of my teenagers, you can't do five things at once. In fact, when you're paying attention to a customer, you want to make certain that you're actually paying attention to that customer. You don't want to be Skyping, or talking on your phone, or even talking to more than one person at a time. Your customers are the people that are paying for your product or service, and sharing the experience of doing so. I learned in a difficult way, just how important that can be.

A while back, I shared a booth at the Whole Foods Expo in San Francisco, together with some very successful businesspeople. On this particular day, there were three of us in the booth, and there were probably a thousand or more people at the expo. At one point for a couple of hours, the place just got packed. People were three or four deep at our booth, which was about 12 feet long and 8 feet wide. Of course, that's what we thought we wanted at an expo, interested people, and we were handing out information and explaining things about our products. In the middle of giving out samples and showing people photographs and short videos, to two or three people at a time just to keep the flow going, I noticed that one of the members of our group had taken one potential customer off to the side to talk privately. Mark happened to be a really good businessman, and as we scrambled through the next hour and things started to calm down, I looked over and, sure enough, Mark was still talking to the same person. I could tell through his body language that he was listening very carefully and was genuinely interested in what this person had to say.

Nobody, out of the hundreds of people we had talked to at the booth, bought anything significant over time. They just took the information and didn't really act. But over the next few years, Mark's customer bought thousands and thousands of dollars' worth of products from us, making Mark a lot of money in the process.

That was a painful way I had to learn that one customer at a time is really important, and to really pay attention. I only had to learn once and it was still expensive. I've seen Mark model that behavior time and time again—somebody is interested and he starts to really listen and ask the right questions to find the solution. Get away from the crowd and don't be interrupted by all the other noise that's going on around you.

Providing people with a life-changing experience, like really being heard and understood in the meantime, is only possible after you've focused on your customers, connected, and discovered what they want.

Chapter 6

Have You Created a Signature Move?

"If you are a female and ask Warren Buffett, the billionaire investor, for a photo with him, he will immediately ask for your hand in marriage."

– The Washington Post

People will remember you and your business, but the question is: for how long, and what for? People sometimes remember other people before experiences, so they will remember you and the people who work with you for the experience they had. An idea my team and I have spent a lot of time with is that your business can be known for a specific thing you do that sets you apart from the crowd —your Signature Move.

A Signature Move is something you're known for, a shared personal connection that your customers start to spread around—a unique way you do business that could well represent your company's entire philosophy. Your Signature Move lets your customers know that when they work with you, they are in for a Signature Experience, something they won't get anywhere else. A Signature Move could be a story that goes around about how you changed somebody's life or just made a much better day for them. What unique experience does your customer remember you for?

It could be, and very often is, how you treat your customers. Here's the key: When most of your customers begin to have the Signature Experience that is unique to your business, that's when the magic of your Signature Move comes in.

You can nurture a Signature Experience that will focus your business on great results. It can start as something simple but powerful, like genuine, heartfelt gratitude expressed in a sincere smile and appreciation for your customers. It can then continue as concrete steps you take to let your customers hear, feel, and see your appreciation, and it can finally manifest as a Signature Experience your customers have when using your product or service.

Companies of all sizes do this. One of my favorite examples can be found in the legend of Nordstrom, an upscale department store. I drove 300 miles and visited Nordstrom in Portland, Oregon, just this past week just to reacquaint myself with the experience.

Nordstrom is legendary in the customer experience business (there's even a book about it called *The Nordstrom Way*), and their Signature Move exemplifies what they're all about. This story is about the Signature Experience customers often have when they shop at Nordstrom.

This story has been recounted in many ways, but the version I know is that many years ago, a woman was very unhappy with a set of tires that Nordstrom had put on her car. She thought they were too noisy, so she brought in her tires, stacked them up against the wall next to Nordstrom's return counter, and advised the clerk that she didn't like the tires and wanted her money back. The clerk looked at the price of the tires, reached into the till, and gave her the money back. After writing up a receipt, he thanked her for coming in and invited her back to shop at Nordstrom.

So was the Signature Move here handling a return? Nope.

The signature move has to do with the fact that Nordstrom doesn't sell tires.

Nordstrom's Signature Move is to fully meet their customer's needs, whatever those may be.

Now, that is a story that's been shared for many years about Nordstrom. I have been told that story for at least a dozen years. It's what got me to visit there in the first place, and my experiences since that time have been wonderful.

When I was practicing as a landscape architect, I also stumbled upon a Signature Move for my business. Several years back, I landed a very desirable landscape design job in Boulder, Colorado, for about $50,000. This was a significant job, with a big lot. The homeowners and I worked on the design for weeks. After it was approved, I got all of the necessary permits and scheduled a particular week in the summer when construction was going to happen.

The schedule was that on Monday, guys were going to grade the landscape and put in the berms. On Tuesday, 60 to 70 large rocks, which came out to 110 *tons* of boulders, would be delivered (one of these boulders was the size of a Volkswagen). Wednesday would be the day for digging trenches for the sprinkler system, and Thursday the sprinkler system would be set up and the boulders would be put in their places with a gigantic 100-foot tall crane. Plants and trees would go in on Friday, and finally on Saturday, I had scheduled putting down a quarter-acre carpet of absolutely beautiful bluegrass sod. This was all set up months in advance.

But when the Friday before we were supposed to do all of this came, I started said, "We can't do it next week. We're just booked, and we're not going to get there." I was pulling my hair out trying to think of a way to pull this off. As it turned out, they could all be there on Saturday, but I was thinking what a mess it would be to have literally 20 people, 10 trucks, and cranes and tractors everywhere, all on the same day.

Then this little light went on. I didn't have any room in the schedule to do it any other way, and I was determined to get the job done. So that Saturday morning, starting at 7:00 a.m., all of these contractors and their help starting showing up with tractors, dump trucks, ditch witches, sod, rock, and trees and bushes. Everything.

I was in a bit of a panic, waving my arms and yelling at this guy, yelling at that, and getting people out of the way, and at some point, about two hours into this, I looked over—and this is a very upscale neighborhood—and there are half a dozen neighborhood kids standing there watching this whole thing.

There were rocks swinging through the air, geysers from the sprinkler system going in, mud everywhere, people slipping and sliding around, people trying to adjust rocks, laying down sod, putting in trees and yelling. It was just an amazing mess. And the neighborhood kids were just loving it.

Around noon, about five hours into the craziness, not only were there more kids watching, but there were pare*nts* there also. So the crew all kind of sat down for a quick sandwich, and I said to the crew, "You know, we're putting on a show here." And we were going to be working until dark. "So for this afternoon, let's just really go for it. Let's really put on a show."

And these guys really got into it. That was a huge yard, probably at least two-thirds of an acre, and a quarter of an acre of that was lawn. We put on this incredible show where there were rocks swinging and people yelling and people pushing dirt into different places and sculpting the yard, and it was just an amazing thing. At times, there were 20 neighbors standing around out in the street watching this whole thing go down. It certainly didn't hurt my relationship with my customers. By the time we rolled out that carpet of sod at about 8:00 p.m., we got a standing ovation from these people. We had the best time.

And the reason I tell this is because it became my Signature Move. From then on, whenever I had a big design back in the '80s, I'd schedule it all in one day and that was part of the contract with my contractors. I'd say, "Look, this is the day. You gotta be there." We'd always start early on Saturday morning, and we would bring out people from all over town, and we would put on a show. It was almost like a zoo or a carnival. The neighborhood would always have a fantastic experience.

And I would get more jobs that way. Within a week or two of doing one job, it was not uncommon to get two or three jobs every time as a direct result of the first. I'd get a call: "Yeah, we want ours done." They wanted the design, they wanted the service, and they wanted the quality, but they also wanted a show at their place. They wanted an experience. So that became my signature way of doing business and I really enjoyed it, along with many of my clients. It was our Signature Move and a Signature Experience for my clients.

The last story I want to relate about Signature Moves is something a little more serious, or at least it was to me when I was first told it in my twenties. It was a story about this man and his family who moved from Arkansas and eventually to northern California during the Depression. The man had a gas station, and he repaired radios, cars and eventually airplanes. At first they made it to the Los Angeles area in the '30s, and it was just really tough going. Over time they migrated to northern California. He was just another guy that worked really hard. It was a tough economic time so he was often doing work for people who couldn't pay. They desperately needed their cars to get to work, so he would say something like, "Well, when you get the money, pay me." Everybody did their best. And so, around 10 years later, he had this large cigar box full of these IOUs of what he was owed. The stack of slips was two inches thick, and quietly one day this man took that cigar box full of receipts out behind his repair shop, emptied it in the burning barrel and just burned them.

My father told me this story. He told me he was in tears because it represented literally tens of thousands of dollars (a huge sum of money at the time). His father, my grandfather, had burned those receipts. They'd been scraping by for a long time and my father just could not figure out why he would do that. But the real story here is that from that day on for the next thirty years of his life, my grandfather never needed to advertise for work. He always had work, and he was always paid well. He ended up owning airplanes and expensive cars, and going big game hunting all over the world on all the business that he always had after that. Because his customers knew that he cared about them, and they just came back and brought their families with them for 30 years.

That was a Signature Move. And you have to believe that those customers had a signature experience they would always remember.

What do your customers know you for beyond your product or service? It can be almost anything, but make it something they can only experience when they work with you and your business. Decide what you want your business to represent, and then incorporate that value into every facet of your company. Customers will come to look forward to the Signature Experience they can have with you.

Chapter 7

What Exactly Is Word of Mouth And Why Is It So Important Right Now?

Word-of-mouth advertising is the most powerful form of advertising, and actually the only consistently effective form of advertising that there is for continued business success. When I have a successful—or unsuccessful—interaction with another business's product or service, I'll tell friends, family, or business associates about that experience. And based on that firsthand story from me, they may become either more or less likely to use that product or service. Word of mouth is so important because the main thing that people pay attention to is their friends, their family, and their colleagues about what businesses and services to use.

You can inspire your customers to tell everyone about your business in a few ways. When you give Kick-Ass Customer Service and people feel important and heard while they're at your business, they want to tell their friends. The strategies in this book will help you deliver the customer service they're looking for. Ask yourself: Did you answer their questions fully? Did you pay attention and really focus on your customer? Were you more interested than interesting? Did your customer have the kind of experience you want them bragging to their friends about?

Remember, you want to pay careful attention to who is in front of you, not to your messages, your phone or some other distraction. By really focusing on the person in front of you, customers will notice and start your word-of-mouth advertising "campaign" for you, because when somebody feels important, that's the experience they will talk about.

Word-of-mouth advertising costs you the price of doing a great job for your customers and nothing less. You listen carefully, you attend to your customer's needs, and you help them find a solution in a signature way. The word of mouth is going to be great, and that is free advertising that more than pays for itself.

Word of mouth might seem to be a well-guarded secret because so few businesses practice the principles that make it so effective. They are simple principles but very effective:

1. Continually over-satisfy your customers and they will spread the word about their experience and your business.
2. Supply your customers with the tools and knowledge to help them spread the word about your business and teach them how to do it.

What can you do to stoke your word-of-mouth advertising right away?

Get out from behind your desk and meet your customers

Short term, one of the things you can do to stoke your word-of-mouth advertising is to go to your customers; don't wait for them to come to you. Let's say you own a winery—your customers may be coming to taste your wines. But you can also go out and connect with them as they're walking around your tasting room. You don't have to wait for them to come ask you questions about your products; you can offer them the information they are looking for. Remember to serve and educate first.

Ask your customers what they want

As we've discussed from the beginning, talking to your customers about what they want, asking them where they're from, or asking them if you can get them anything is one of the first steps you want to take. When you know what they want, you can then begin educating them about the best options to meet and exceed their needs. It all starts with a question.

Both of these are great ways to get started, but how do you build this into an effective word-of-mouth strategy for the long term?

The Story of Your Business

One of the most powerful ways that you can build a long-term strategy is to have a story about your business. What inspired you to make the move? What obstacles did you overcome? But remember, you can't start telling this to your customers one on one until they feel valued and appreciated by you.

So, learn your customers' stories: where they're from, why they're there, and what they like. When you begin to learn those things about your customer, when they begin sharing their story, they will want to hear yours. By providing Kick-Ass Customer Service, your customers will want to go home and talk about what a great experience and amazing time they had with you. Once you begin to have customers having those types of experiences, they're going to start telling your story.

For a long-term advertising strategy, there's not a more powerful option than providing customer service, every time that they'll remember. And don't be afraid to ask your customers to tell their friends about the experience they had with you— once you've created that connection, they'll be happy to recommend you. Kick-Ass Customer Service has the power to transform your word-of-mouth advertising campaign.

Are You Ready to Get Started?

You now have the tools you need to start transforming your business with Kick- Ass Customer Service. With these strategies, you can propel your business to new heights.

We've covered a lot in this short book, so before you head out to implement the steps, take a second to look at the Kick-Ass Customer Service Principles:

Kick-Ass Principles

Know What Your Customer Actually Wants

✓ Ask your customer what outcome they are looking for
✓ Develop a clear mental picture of their desired outcome
✓ Be the leader and organize the solution

Inspire Employees to Perform as Ambassadors

✓ Inspire your employees to act like ambassadors
✓ Be clear that you're all in business to serve your customers
✓ Exceed your customer's expectations

Educate Your Customers, Don't Sell Them

✓ Educate, don't sell, by looking for solutions
✓ Ask questions to help clarify your customer's vision

✓ Repeat the vision to your customer until you are both clear

Feel Gratitude and Show Your Appreciation

✓ Express your gratitude and show customers your appreciation
✓ Make a connection with your customers
✓ Model the behavior you want your employees to copy

Offer Your Customers a Life-Enhancing Experience First, Then Graduate to a Life-Changing Experience

✓ Find out why your customers have chosen your business

✓ Ask them how you can make their experience of your business better
✓ Focus on one customer at a time

Focus On Creating a Signature Experience for Your Customers

✓ Set your business apart from the crowd
✓ Create a Signature Move from shared, personal connections with customers
✓ Offer your customers a Signature Experience

Learn How Word of Mouth Works and How to Leverage It

✓ Create opportunities to connect with your customers
✓ Over-satisfy your customers
✓ Build a story about your business

Keeping every customer that walks through the door, and attracting new ones, is one of the biggest secrets of success in business. What goals will you achieve once you have all the customers you want?

www.ingramcontent.com/pod-product-compliance
Lightning Source LLC
LaVergne TN
LVHW040932150826
845672LV00007B/2318

* 9 7 9 8 4 7 0 6 3 0 3 5 3 *